Other Titles by Peter Weltner

Fiction

Beachside Entries/Specific Ghosts
Identity and Difference
In a Time of Combat for the Angel
The Risk of His Music
How the Body Prays
The Return of What's Been Lost

Poetry

News from the World at My Birth: A History
Laguna Beach: After Shelter
From a Lost Faust Book
From a Lost Gospel of Mark
The One-Winged Body
Where Everything Is Water As Far As He Can See
Water's Eye
The Outerlands
To the Final Cinder
Stone Altars
Late Summer Storm in Early Winter
The Light of the Sun Become Sea

Peter Weltner grew up in New Jersey and North Carolina, graduated from Hamilton College, received a Ph.D. from Indiana University, taught English Renaissance poetry and prose and modern and contemporary British, Irish, and American fiction and poetry at San Francisco State for thirty seven years, and retired in 2006. He lives with his husband in San Francisco by the Pacific.

UNBECOMING TIME

To the Memory of Three Master Teachers

Edwin Barrett
(Shakespeare)

John Crossett
(English Renaissance Poetry and Prose)

John Mattingly
(Latin and Classical Aesthetic Theory and
Mythology in the Renaissance)

Of education all the grace,
Which makes high both the art and place
Of general wonder.

Gower in Act IV of Shakespeare's *Pericles*

ISBN: 978-0-692-97619-7

Published by Marrowstone Press
Copyright, 2017

Cover Image: 'The Transmogrification of Robert Stark,'
photograph by Galen Garwood, 2017

UNBECOMING TIME

Poems

PETER WELTNER

Marrowstone Press

Table of Contents

V

I

New Year's Day, the First Hours

Seconds before midnight,
only a few stars shine
round a sliver of the moon
in a flat matte black sky
that at twelve explodes
into fiery sparklers, fountains,
spiralling rockets,
the racket an attack
on coal-eyed tar-faced red-tongued demons
that riotous cacophony casts back to hell.

Torches glowing
where they stand
along the strand,
bonfires dimly burning,
revelers seeking sleep,
longing for a deeper night,
sinking into dreams
now evil's kept at bay,
the beach a safe haven
while the tide is low for a few more hours.

I, you, my love, two old men
strolling late along the sea,
by night's nether side,
the dark that awaits us,
the ocean char black,
stars, moon having set
below a vanished horizon,
while sky, water flow as one
toward oblivion,
the obvious world.

New Year's Day, Dawn

Reborn, the Pacific is calm
at lowest tide.
Gray, drifting clouds. A psalm-
like tune is sung beside
the shoreline. As dawn rises slowly
over the hills, the horizon
gleams pale gold. A rite to Laka
is being performed, a ceremony done
in obeisance to Hawaii,
by first light's aqua
sky, to life and the sea.
Boys, girls dance for the islands, its waters,
as waves dance, wear-
ing bright red flowers
in their wind-swept hair.

New Year's Day, Noon

An old man, his hair
like mop strings wrung dry, white,
frayed, his skin so faded and palely fair
his skull sticks through it. He is no sight
for your eyes to enjoy on the year's first day. What fantasies
he erases in you, the past, youthful bodies,
one night stands, orgies, sprees,
a long ago yesterday
you are better off no longer recalling. Try to say
something kind to him. He has lost
the good of his mind but not his gai-
ety. He is singing on a dune. Or some ghost
of him is. Dancing, prancing, dar-
ing you mock him while watching him teach you why you should care.

New Year's Day, Late Afternoon

This should be no place to learn silence.
Waves crack like ice floes
breaking. Near sunset,

the wind's a perpetual violence
like a long winter storm's.
The seawall's breached and wet.

With apparently no notion
of the danger he's in,
a kitesurfer flies over the sea.

Whitecaps rise and crash on the ocean
as far as the horizon,
the sun bulbous, clown-face ruddy.

A squall-force gust lifts him up
still higher, carries him over
dunes toward the highway

where the wind means to drop
him, kite deflated, onto the asphalt
for a car to slay

or a pickup truck. Plovers scurry
in ritual circles
mimicking a dirge

above the pounding of the waves, the lee-
ward shrieking of gulls,
their flight a surge

like the sea's as its waves overflow
the sand-slick busy road.
It's his, this astonished quiet, the silence

sudden in the stillness afterward,
after people's screams, brakes' screeching,
a racing ambulance,

a cop car's sirens. The winds have died. The ocean
no longer protests. Time's been subsided,
suspended, is in abstention.

His, the kitesurfer's, the quiet of sun
and sky, the hush of his girlfriend's
breathless mute ululation

after she has heard the news, what has been done
to them the first day of the year,
who are nothing now. No one. No one.

New Year's Day, Evening

1.

Two hawks fly over the bluffs, climb
higher to perch in a Monterey pine.

A precipice. Sheer cliffs. Boulders
battered by encroaching waters.

Pelicans appear from nowhere, fly-
ing through mist into a darkening sky.

Hikers pass by toward Land's End,
read signs, vanish around the bend.

2.

The couple's old as are their friends.
A late life marriage before life ends.

Here, by the Gate, foghorns moan
like Russian basses their ritual drone.

Like a river in a Noh play, a long, white
cloth's been laid on the ground for the bride.

A guitar's played, vows pledged. All shiver
from a wind blowing eastward in winter.

3.

The trees' bark has been blackened by hard rain.
Evening shadows their faces. They kiss again.

Applause. A few cheers. A gull caws
as it heads for the bridge. A long pause.

The time nears its end. To begin a new life
on the year's first day as husband and wife.

To live as if we can know what love is.
What it gives or denies. Why sometimes it suffices.

Cinders' Dust

When I was little we still had a coal bin.
Imagine that. And a coal furnace in
the basement. And coal ash like grimy
snow on roads, soft, gray as sea
foam piled in a corner of the base-
ment I played in until I looked
like a dirty snowman or a ghost that spooked
me. Imagine that dark place
when I saw my clothes, my face
in a mirror covered with flakes of ash,
the skin below it like a boy with a rash
as if I'd been rolling in snow or burned
beyond knowing. So much might be learned
from ashes. Imagine a child. What fires can erase.

Another Life

It's always dawn when I hear Jay's fear
during his last call to me, painful
every time, his whispering, coughing
still clear almost forty years later.

This morning, two surfers rescued a boy
from drowning. I walk the beach staring
as others ride their boards to shore
and quickly paddle back out again.

It's not that paradise is always a lie.
Or a fantasy. Like Tiberius's island,
Capri was the name of a bar where I'd go
after I'd come out late looking for pleasure.

The Stud. The Lion. The Rendezvous.
The seedy, sweat-drenched Rawhide.
Most of the men I knew then have died.
Every day I think of them. And Jay.

My ways have become ordinary. I live
in a beachside neighborhood in a house
that rests on sand near where Playland
once stood. Or I live in old memories.

I watched a film last night. A woman
was hanged unjustly in such terror
she needed to be doped and carried
to the scaffold. She'd had romantic dreams.

That she'd be happier than she was,
that the aurora borealis might shine nightly
in every sky, spring would never die,
and she'd live another life like this, but better.

Yadkin River

1.

After a night's steady rain,
the Carolina sky is a slick slate gray
marbled with slivers of clouds
that at dawn glow with the wet-brick color
of piedmont clay.
Say it suffices, the sounds
of birdsong and squirrels
and locust after a storm,
the river rising, blood red
as if a god's done it great harm.

2.

The moon reflects on the river
like a wanderer
pursuing a journey,
the moving, rippling water
breaking its light
into thousands of pieces
silvery as fish scales
or glittering coins
the night releases
like the gold poured on Danaë from Zeus' loins.

3.

The river as Word, its swift currents,
signs posted on bridges warning
of sudden floods. Moans, laments
heard from nearby woods:
a hoarse breathing,
a shrieking hurricane wind
that casually slaughters
some of the forest's primeval trees,
the ghosts they invoke of,
oh, the lord of the world and all its waters.

4.

Summer's belief in divinities,
in boys, stripped to their boxers
or briefs, diving, swimming,
treading water in the Yadkin,
basking on its grassy banks,
grateful for the sun rippling through leaves
drying their wet hair, warming their skin,
the day growing hotter,
more holy as, like a lover,
it enfolds them, bold and timeless as the river.

Five Aquariums

Their five filters incessantly gurgle. The room fills with sun
through two dormers in the morning waking the boy up. He's grown.
The world's beckoning him like a friend he wouldn't have known
or recognized, so much it has changed. Last Sunday after church, alone,
he'd watched a jay he'd hoped he had saved breathing its last
in his lap and buried it in his backyard. The mournful child
he likes to play daily visits its grave beneath a tree. He's compiled
a journal of sorts of his losses. Grandparents. His steadfast
best friend. Two dogs. Cousin Luke. Yesterday in a crazed fit
a silken blue Siamese fighting fish broke free and sicced
a dwarf gourami, bloodied its eyes and fins, and bit
off its tail. Late March, his fire mouthed cichlids all died from ich.
He had flushed them down the toilet one by one. The beautiful
survivors he continues to feed each day before he leaves for school.

A Pastoral Childhood

1.

A boy's reading Hemingway on the green
quad of a college near his home, his back
propped on the trunk of a live oak
whose thick leaves shade him, a canopy
upholding the sky. Hidden, unseen
by teachers, a bumblebee attack-
ing him, he thinks of a joke
he likes and laughs a little. See
how happy he is, alone,
sitting on dew-damp grass,
reading, dozing, imagining
the future, what he'll have done
some day. A flock of geese pass
over head. Watch him watching everything.

2.

The sun rises higher over the college,
its chapel's steeple aflame in the light.
Its bells ring it is time to change
classes, its tones deep and clear.
The boy envies the knowledge
of professors, good students. He catches sight
of an older boy who smiles back. Strange
how his looks make reading dear-
er. The Sun Also Rises. Clouds
are fast forming. Soon it'll rain.
He puts his book under
his jacket. Paris. The crowds
in Pamplona. Again.
To be there again. To care for life like a writer.

3.

He's drenched as he walks home
on the shoulder of an old country
road, but his books stay dry.
The storm's left everything
he sees luminous. He would say, Come
join me. This is what life ought to be,
at peace with itself and the earth. Why
shouldn't I remain here? The sky's like a ring
round the world, the air
thick with magnolia, honey-
suckle, the trees' leaves steaming,
petals glowing sunward. Dare
to know me, he pleads to someone. We
two, in this shine things emit, by June's ripe gleaming.

Two Late Pastorals

1. The Garden

My father planted many thriving shrubs
on his land, euonymous, osmansis,
nandina, ligustrum, boxwood. Some grew
window-high and blocked out the light.

The lawn was crowded with trees. Dogwood,
redbud, pin oak, loblolly pine,
deodar cedar, gum trees that dropped
devil's pincushions onto the ground.

I'd pick them up in an old yellow sheet
or carry them in a basket to a gully.
Pfitzer and creeping juniper lined
walls and walks. Pyracantha, forsythia,

jasmine, camellias, cerise and scarlet
azaleas, gardenias, pink indicas,
gardenia, rhododendron competed with
hydrangea, crepe myrtle, lilacs for space.

He kept his bird feeders filled with suet
and seed for the towees, wood thrushes,
bluejays, blackbirds, and cardinals
that perched in trees or on backyard wires.

One summer day, when I was fourteen,
I went outside to watch the afternoon
sun glitter on leaves and needles like light
on a pool seen from under water

and found in woods behind the house
the corpse of a dog, its gray skin split
by the sun, ants crawling on its ears and eyes
that, though cloudy, stayed open as if alive.

I should have told the truth about my life
when I could. I should have made less
of it lies. This is a story about my father.
How he tended his garden. How I watched him die.

2. *The Beach*

Dozens of migrating pelicans,
a few geese, some plovers, a tribe
of white and gray gulls are feeding
by the shoreline on tiny fish the tide

brings in. The sea's calm after
days of rough currents and high waves.
Some sleekly feathered, bolder geese
swim or float in the water as in

a pond while pelicans circle above them,
their long, wide wings seldom flapping,
gliding in the gentle winds, their beaks
like thin, slightly curved scissors' blades.

Most of the others seem to be waiting,
patient as birds carved from wood,
as if after such a feast they must take
their leave of this beach and fly far off.

I would say they are staring out to sea.
I would say they are observing a rite
unknown to mankind. Like a prayer,
perhaps, or some way of offering thanks.

People walking their dogs off leash
pay them no mind, let them run
where they will, playing, barking,
chasing after, pursuing their prey.

Like one, the frightened birds soar away
in a roar of flapping like a gust of wind
from a sudden storm, disappearing
northward to some place I'll never see

like a fantasy, the dream I hold dearest
fading into the sky. Like you.
Like the beach we made love on. The lies
we denied. My betrayal far clearer than you are.

Swimmer in a Storm

In the lull between torrents, more lightning,
the acrid odor of burned air,
the smell of wet dead flowers, frightening
in a way, the scent of someone no longer there

or the stench of moldy cement. The rumbling
of thunder. Winds swirling pine cones, petals,
twigs–all spiraling like leaves, tumbling
to earth, littering the ground. The calls

of wild creatures silenced. The swells
of steam that fog the streets. The shudder
of woods, chattering, chanting old spells
to ward off more scary weather. The danger,

the brunt of its power yet to come.
Not safety he craves, not comfort, home,
but him, heron, egret, snake,
rising as reeds do, like mist from the lake

as clouds regather, amassing, black
as wet ashes, a glow, a steel sheen
to air a sulfur yellow smoke stack
color, the grass a fern or algae green.

Then rain falling harder, flooding farms,
creeks, overflowing streams, and he
getting wetter while staring at arms
splashing through water, slowly, strongly

stroking, the swimmer–like spillway, bird wing,
water lily–defiant, reckless despite
the charge in the sky, the deluge swamping
the earth, the risk, the thrill that light-

ning might strike the lake, the throbbing air,
thunderbolts, rushing water,
crashing, gale-like winds: not despair
but the joys of a boy who's never been happier.

A Summer Dawn, Darkly Breaking

The clouds that fill the sky are the pale gray
of thin wet snow on stones. The sea's
the gray of tarnished tin. Let the day
be what you mean. Let dismal weather seize
the soul that needs it. Sailing westward,
a cargo ship looks pencilled in.
Wet suits like ink spots. The mist toward
the north obscures the hills, veiled as with rain.
Waves break, gray as old torn sheets.
The sand's a brownish gray like stripped timber
tossed aside, sun-faded. Gray as sleet's
the seawall, the highway gray as worn rubber.
Oh, gray tears of a child staring out a window
at the face of a boy who would share his sorrow.

The Future of an Illusion

It's a muggy morning, minutes after first light.
Clouds and fog mingle to form a mountain,
vast and imposing, over the horizon. Like sight-
ing an island risen from the sea through rain,
unsure what it means, he stands and stares. Fishermen
watch with him at water's edge, as if anticipating
strange travelers sailing here, no one knows when.
A black trawler and a heavy cargo ship are heading
toward the port of a secluded town the Pacific's
concealing while the sun lifts higher, shining
a pink-gray light throughout the sky. What tricks
the mind likes to play. The scene fades to nothing.
It's full day. He looks at his wrinkled, bony hands.
What would he see there? Another country. Unknown lands.

II

Something Understood

When I was a boy, funerals were no place
for children. I was left at home to play
with friends. First grandmother Karen
died, then Louise. Gone, leaving no trace,
as if one day they'd vanished. I'd pray
they'd return to me. Fruitless prayers, barren
hopes. I stand on a hill of Bay View Cemetery
in Jersey City, a park, docks, the Hudson
below me. It's not what we ask of the dead
but what they ask of us that makes
us who we are. The river enters the sea,
emptying into it, as if its life were done
as ours must be at the end, having said
what we could. Cargo ships, a cruise liner
plow into the North Atlantic. To suffer
departure. What an ocean gives, it takes
back. I'm watching its heedless flowing,
feeling the tides, the currents of my dying
inside me, the emptiness of it, my life bidden
to it. Not mine but my father's. "My son, my son."

Eucharist

I walk each day by the sea,
gazing at its vast, anonymous graveyard,
grieving like a widow
whose husband drowned off this coast years ago,
wondering what he or I
or anyone might say to others knowing
death must take him soon,
this afternoon perhaps,
what it might mean to ask
of your friends before you die
who will survive you,
to give them the task,
or maybe the favor
of transforming mourning into liturgy
as Jesus at his seder did,
requesting they eat bread, drink wine
in memory of me,
he said
as if any of them could forget
the death he gave them, the life they'd lost.

Angsumnes

1.

A storm raging, the earth rescinding its blessing,
a torrential rain demonstrating what little remains
of safety, trees undone by surges, gusts cling-
ing to branches shaking like prisoners rattling their chains.

2.

Circumlocutory. The day following, laying word upon word,
stone upon stone, as if erecting more fortified walls,
language's mortar and bricks, an absurd
bulwark ruined, toppled by brute gales or squalls.

3.

Seaweed the hurricane has tossed onto the beach, nerves
like tangled threads and wires, scattered
on sand. Longing, or what lingers
of it, the crushed houses, piers desire saves, reserves
to show in the aftermath, bodies shattered,
lying on shore, the shock of fucking's battered, beaten down borders.

Matins

For years, I've watched an elderly Chinese
couple each day faithfully walking by the sea.
As I'd reach near them, to please
the three of us, perhaps too freely,
I'd say, "Hello. Good morning." They'd smile,
nod, and silently pass by. Up the coast,
once, striding in their usual single file,
they faded into dense fog like a ghost.
Now they've disappeared forever. Where?
Did one die? Or both move? It was nothing
much, of course. But it felt important, rare,
my words, their smiles, our ceremony of greeting.
Such a loss. Oh, I know. You say, All things flow.
And they do. But I miss the ritual I made-up to follow.

Sea Blue

1.

A flawed, slightly cracked aquamarine glass goblet
rests on the living room mantle, patiently waiting
for the sun each morning to spill into it, flow through it,
painting sea blue a wall and the cloudy, chalk-white ceiling.

2.

In the Bahamas, a lifeguard wades into water
that is a serene turquoise and stabs and spears
black sea porcupines he throws in his sack. The slaughter
turns the sea's blue to scarlet from blood the high tide clears.

3.

Naked except for boxer shorts the same
sea blue of his irises, Nick strums
a guitar in his dorm room, hums
to the tune. A tooth is chipped from a hockey game.
His yellow hair flops over one eye.
Desire. The sea's blue or Jarman's blinded blue or Hiroshige's rainy sky.

Gray

1.

The great gray monster in his dreams
stomping down halls, thudding on floors,
always about to, never reaching the room
where, sleeping, he stifles his screams.
On a drab, stormy morning, rain streams
over gutters. Winds pound on doors.
Dawn is as gray as the stones of a tomb.
An imprisoning day. A day of extremes.
He traces the raindrops
on windows with his fingers.
The storm never stops.
The panes are cold. Winter's
closing in. There's no running away.
He's only a child, warned it's dangerous to stray.

2.

The beach is deserted. Smoke grows
more acrid downwind from a smoldering fire.
The water is a glistening olive gray,
gray as flat slate where the wind blows
hardest, the sky a smudged charcoal that glows
like white cinders the higher he looks. To tire
of life. To know every day
he approaches death closer. What the sea shows
through fog, barely visible:
a coal black ship drifting westward,
sea, clouds indistinguishable
from the horizon it is slowly heading toward,
the sun as it rises always
behind it, shrouded in morning's mortal gray haze.

A Solitary Surfer at Dawn

Once more this morning I'm walking beachside
by the Pacific imagining as I did in last night's dream
a city under the sea waiting
to rise a second time on an island wide
as a flotilla seen from shore. The ocean glitters like a stream
that's crystalline blue, like a thin covering
of ice on a lake in early winter
that conceals what lies below, submerged in deep water.

A surfer steps into the surf,
paddles out on his board,
the first to awaken, to rise
before dawn from sleep for a ride that is worth
living for, the spell of the surge that lies
beneath his feet, the force of waves that spur him sunward.

Two Sculptures Built from Driftwood
in Memory of a Friend Who Drowned

One piece could be a woman who's tossed her wet hair
over her face for the sun to dry, its twigs
and loose tree limbs dangling from a thick, bare
branch, swinging in the sea breeze like sprigs
of flowers or the stems of new plants. Stones
encircle it, like cairns or ruins of runes. The other,
simpler, is a branch like a stretched-out S or a crone's
crookéd spine delicately balanced on a tall water-
worn log to form a crude cross. From a distance
a knob on the stake's top resembles a hawk,
perched, looking for prey. Their work had no chance
of lasting, its builders knew. Today, when I walk
the beach, all its pieces are gone, swept away by the sea,
like a sand painting scattered by breezes, a caged beast set free.

Two Dream Pictures by Galen Garwood

1.

Unbound by land, an ancient lake that lies
as wide and open as a sea
burns as if from a bonfire
that is raging on it or that randomly flames
from leaves or newspaper. What gives their names
to the world are the fires of change. The sky's
bleak, dark as night or darkly cloudy.
Stones might burn as this water does,
spontaneously combusting, too, as desire
ignites from the heat of a body
in its fervor, its ardor.
See how the fire comes, sleepless
in dream, night made profounder
by the sea you sink into, saying, unknowingly, Yes.

2.

Elemental transfigurations. See, too, how love's
blazing from the surface of a lake,
an inland sea, from which a lover
from twenty years before
rises out of its flickering water
naked, boldly enticing, muscular—
as from slighter flames a rebel solider soars, hovers
from the sky over all below, his face stricken by war,
his smoldering eyes prophetic of his death,
the deaths of the thousand thousand others
left, abandoned, forsak-
en, bleeding, in merciless
battles, Shiloh, Cold Harbor,
the Wilderness.

3.

Hudor, pyrá, ancient Greek
words I summon here
to invoke the metamorphoses
of memory,
the anywhere
that dream can be, take place, by which I seek
to see
through two men in two photographs the primal traces
of a dark and light
that's lost to day and its betrayals but recalled at night,
by which I mean to say in the pyres of a sea,
in the mystery
of art, of what's reborn: A lover known. A soldier being
mourned. And water burned and burning.

Sentinel

A northern cold, harshly bitter,
the moon hazily
haloed. Rain or snow soon. Fear water,
night's silence, a sea
that's no guide, frightening
in its enormity.

He concentrates. Waits. There's nothing
to see but ocean and sky,
both pitch black though in patches bruised
a dark purple blue
like a man abused
and beaten. Spindrift blows
salt on his face. His clothes
are icy. A solitary sailor, lookout for his slumbering crew.

For Saint Lucy's Night and Ceremonies of Peace

Moonlight seen through thin clouds' silvery sheen.
Waves soaring twenty feet high or higher,
roaring like a cascade. Rock-bound tide pools glitter-
ing, mirroring stars. The ocean's a wild Saint Vitus
dance. Swirling winds. Whitecaps careen-
ing, clashing. A pungent scent blows in off the water
from charred driftwood, seaweed, the blight
of trash, fish bones, dead crabs, toxic rotting refuse.

Northern breezes sweep in late, sweetening the air.
It is Saint Lucy's Night, a rite
for winter. In their plaited hair
crowned by wreaths, girls in white
bring alms, carry candles they have lit
to still the dark's cold, storm-like spirit.

Early Morning

Whitewater, gulls' breasts, the crests
of dunes, black wet suits,
a plaque on the promenade: all blaze
like a mirror the sun's shining on.

A red hawk, its eyes glaring,
rests on a wire. The ocean
glitters like rhinestones. Plovers,
scattering, greet the dawn.

What hurled us here from what
far star? Light, more radiant
than this fiery morning,
desire dazzling the world.

Elderly Fishermen at Dawn

1.

The rising sun burns the tumbling white water
a flaming yellow as it rushes to shore.
A woman with tangled red hair, claw-like lavender
nails wails on the sea walk against the war.
Leaning on its wall, two surfers argue about
the best waves to ride off Patagonia's
coast. A dog barks gruffly, trying to rout
a conspiracy of ravens, then sits to lick its paws.

2.

Elderly fishermen in waders wait
for the lines of their poles planted
in sand to tighten from fish caught
on baited hooks. To count on fate
more than skill. To be content, fed
by the sea, all their lines suddenly taut.

Tradition

The night is stormy, the house perched on
a bluff. A rough sea is rising fast.
All these elements he knows. It's an old, hoary
story, after all, in a long derided style.
How he returns to his home alone,
pounds on a locked door with his fist,
pleads to be allowed to enter. How his family
or whoever inhabits it now only sigh
as they hide in windows, floorboards, drapery,
furniture, mirrors, repeatedly deny-
ing him entry. Ill, soaked by saltwater
and rain, provoked, he knocks insistently
on the fastened door, still hearing no answer
from the dead he loves and implores to be let in by.

Coastal Diary

Gray as wet rocks, clouds hang heavy
in the sky.
A surprising summer rain is falling.
Who I

am is an old man standing at the edge of a world.
The Pacific's
too wild for surfers today, shining
like a mix

of chrome plate and steel. A fisherman
in waist-high
waders is drenched by waves as he casts his line.
Why

must I leave you, the earth I love? In flocks,
pelicans,
their beaks like awls, fly south over
Land's

End. When I was a child, I nailed
an owl's wings
found in woods to a plank I hung on a wall.
Such things

boys do unknowing of death, the stink, the look
of it,
its feathers rusting like fallen petals or leaves.
I sit

on a stone wall while a ship dredges the ocean
floor
for sand, loading itself with it like a barge
to restore

the beaches last spring's late storms washed
away.
Riptides along the shoreline are leaving a snake's
wavy

patterns on the sand. New driftwood lies by dunes
like bones
from a desert dig. A retriever runs loose, barks,
as if it owns

the coast, the gulls, ravens, plovers, the ball
its human
throws again. My father would feed the birds once winter
began,

suet, seed. Titmice, thrushes, finches,
chickadees,
cardinals. The shells they scattered on snow
were pleas

for more, darkly sparkling like pebbles seen lying beneath
a white sea.
A man wearing plugs in his earlobes,
ratty

cut-offs paws like a dog in the sand for something
he's lost.
A pit-black freighter, loaded with cargo, slips
like a ghost

ship out of the bay into a shroud of distant fog
and disappears.
My friend, here, where a continent completes its journey,
here's

where we'll finish what remains of our days. I am the lake
I swam in
as a boy, the ocean by which I walk each morning,
the din

of the surf I sleep to at night, the water
I've dreamed of
throughout my life, praying something of us might stay
like our love

for each other after we've died. I'm unbecoming time,
as a river,
flooded, overflows its banks, as sunlight
in summer

exceeds every measure, as migrating birds by their flying
empty
without reason the sky, the sea, you, me of all but their flight's
fleet beauty.

Sleeplessness

Past midnight, a surprising storm, the rain
battering windows. At sunrise, incense,
candles still burn behind neighbors'
gates in devotion to their stone Buddhas.

Take care of your ghosts. Offer them
common pleasures. They float over
the world wanting back in. At the beach,
a steel-like smell is stinging the air.

Salt dust encrusts pebbles and rocks,
pieces of crabs' shells. A crow pecks at
a fish's gutted, bony carcass.
A man in waders deftly casts his line.

Mist from high waves hovers over
the highway. Splashing above a wall,
the sea gushes onto streets. Water
spouts from trucks' tires, off boats' hulls.

A rust- and sulfur-colored foam's
drifting, rolling like tumbleweed
across the sand or over dunes,
wherever breezes blow it. The madness,

the fit of humanity in it. The wind's
picking up. The sky's darkening
like my bedroom ceiling late at night
where shadows play while I'm failing sleep.

III

A Birthday Gift

A cooly red rose, cut pink peonies,
a sprig of bluebells in a crystal bowl
half filled with fresh water. A breeze
rustling leaves quietly to console
all fears perhaps, to offer comfort.
After recent storms, there's a change
in weather. Squirrels making sport
by scrambling up and down trunks. A strange,
mangy dog roaming the yard. Chickadees,
flickers, finches, titmice, cardinals
on the wing or singing in bushes or trees.
The neighbor next door who twice calls
to her son. A white linen table cloth.
A clear bottle the sun's shining through
making a rainbow, a prismatic swath
of colors. Unlit candles on a cake. New
birthday cards laid out on the mantel.
Wrapped presents on a counter. It's a date
time tricks you with. The magic, the spell
of Michael still in it. His hesitating, wait-
ing at the door. His unselfish beau-
ty. His oddly sad smile. The gift he's holding
in his arms, embraces tightly, to give you.
And you, never to know why, refusing
it, cruelly confused, acting wantonly
not by design. A scene each birthday
makes you remember, makes you see
as if by repeating it you might fix history.
His happiness. His kiss. Your turning away.

Shame

1.

His father haunts his bedroom late at night,
waiting to argue with him. "What you should
have done you did not do." It's true. Shadows
of his wrongs chase after him. Family. Friends.
There's little time left. His life's not right,
the fiction it's been, neither kind nor good.
Inside him, his ghosts rail and strike blows
against his pride. This is how make-believe ends.

2.

A photograph in a book of an American soldier
mutilated in the battle of Château-Thierry,
his mouth melted, his nose blown off by shells,
his eyelids torn to shreds by wires. The masks
he must wear so no one need be bother-
ed by his scars, to disguise what none should see,
to hide how much he suffers, the endless hells
he's made to descend into, a hero at his tasks.

3.

TV news. A child in a tenement stairwell begging
for food is sent to bed starving.
In the Sonoran desert, refugees are dying.
A battered wife. The hurt a young
girl feels from what a cop insists on calling
an "incident." Villages reduced to nothing.
Cities rent by wars. And language, the house of being,
betrayed by lies spouted each moment in every known tongue.

4.

A raven, a hawk, and a raven perch on a rail
like that, in a row, half-hidden by clumps of sea
grass growing from mounds of sand
that hug the shoulders of The Great Highway.
A trio of birds, not blinking, staring past the pale,
dim light of morning, beyond the horizon, past cre-
ation where no human can look, a land
they peer into deeply and, satisfied, fly to, high and far away.

Self-Portrait in the Guise of a Skull

1.

The Mineshaft. Westside Docks. Raunch bars. The trucks
in the Meatpacking District. Beneath the elevated
West Side highway. Desire enlightened
by rituals, how a man gets fucked or fucks.
A bull whip shoved up an asshole.
Leather masks. Plastic suits. Chains. Racks.
The body garbed in the rôle
it enacts, plays out, to make it shoot.

2.

                           Black's
the dark cave of mortality.
Jerking horn-hard dicks,
too many
to desire even in fantasies. Cruising for tricks,
hook-ups, one night stands. Ecstasy.
Passion. Rapture. No more anyone, him or me.

3.

Eakins' naked boys standing, sitting on a rock
at a wooded lake, the lens
left open for a longer exposure. A photo's a lock
on time, its key twisted, men
who are dying from pleasure, immortal-
ized by a camera the moment the water's
broken.

4.

                        See? All their borders
are violated. Their appall-
ing, shattered beauty, like anemones, calla lilies,
parrot tulips, orchid and leaf loveliest as they die in a white ovoid vase.
Defiant expressions. Outré faces. Who plays
death's part makes love to myriad beauties.

A head floats above a carved skull on the tip of a cane
a right hand grips. The background is lethal:
a withering body outlined by black blank pain.

Again, he says. The dark room. Let me print its pictures again.

Ramrod

1.

The rusty glow of dim streetlights,
fog-gray Victorians, boarded warehouses,
shattered windows, empty stores.
What excites
him, the grim enticements
of narrow alleys, darkness,
skin-slick hide pants, biker's jack-
et, boots' heels clacking on cement.

2.

The Ramrod's brick walls are sooty black,
its iron door studded with nails.
Inside's the rapt scent
of sweat,
spilled booze,
the oak bar he rests
an elbow on, one foot on the rail,
                              chugging a beer.

3.

He's eager for war, for sex's brute conquests,
nothing more real, life never clear-
er or more dear.

4.

                    At the Hot Gates,
their city shamed when they were late for Marathon,
Leonidas and his leather-skinned men fear-
lessly stand in line between stark cliffs, Spartan
warriors commanding the road Persians must pass,
                    taunting their enemies,
                        lovers, side by side,
                            impatiently
awaiting invasion.

Carolina: Free Variations on Poems by Tu Mu

1.

Fifty years. Yesterdays dimming like twilight,
more dark than real. Wind-blown drifts of night.

Dawn breaks over Hanging Rock so finely
I feel no need to climb its heights again.

2.

Scaling the wind scraped mountain
where the trail steepens,
shadows shaped by the sun
hidden behind white clouds,

I paused by a rock ledge
where maple leaves at dusk,
frost-blushed scarlet,
burned bolder than camellia in spring.

3.

A long country highway of oriole, robin songs,
its canopy greenest at dawn,
a crossroads town with hills for walls,
cigarette posters, keen breezes.

Of its one hundred counties'
thousand backwoods churches,
how many steeples tower
above noon's haze of drizzling rain?

4.

Incised in thick moss, a pit that's stolen
its red from a twilight sky.

Later, gray clouds shadow a shadeless window
while a rising moon shines upon shake shingles.

5.

Faraway mountains,
hills shrouded in mist,
moonlight struggling to swim
in a churning river.

Why is he distant tonight,
my friend, so handsome, so good?
Night floods woods.
A creek flows, drowning, into a lake.

6.

I've dallied all day by a brook.
Sunset's a tawny yellow.
A fatality called autumn arrives.
See my sparse white hair?

I've trusted thunderstorms
to clear air, settle dust,
hide August's traces.
A bullfinch sings me northward.

7.

Boys keep tugging at my pants' legs, taunting,
"Why do you take so long to go home?"

I, who watched in the mirror over many lost years
the slow fading away of all I was scared of.

If This Cannot Pass Away Unless I Drink It

1.

Ash gray, chalky white, rippled in patches like sand
by waves at low tide,
this morning's clouds hide
the blue of the sky from hills to horizon.
A thin, long band
of fog hovers below Tam's summit
or looms beside
the headlands, like a strand of smoke vanishing into air
by Bolinas Bay.
The sea is a dark olive green,
the sand black as the ravens that stand
there to stare
with hawk-like eyes at whatever it is they've seen.
They forage for carnage,
hungrily rummag-
ing like bums through trash as gulls strut past and preen.

2.

In the east, an epic rose seeps through the clouds above
Mt. Davidson, tinting the city with a coal's glowing sheen.
The streets are busy early, the sea walk
newly littered with graffiti. The talk
heard, the rumors spread across the land
prophesy dreadful tidings. Sweet merciless love,
bitter, banal,
gray as the sky, gray as the mourning dove
cooing, warbling on a breakwater wall,
say that it is time to submit,
that whoever dies today will be glad of it,
as a pier is happy to be broken by waves,
scattered onto sand,
into the sea,
no more needing to fear
winter storm or summer squall.

Silence as the Art of Departure

1.

Nothing real is possible anymore. Magic
has vanished from the earth, tragedy
has died. (Watch Pasolini's Medea.) The trick
is how to deny it, how to see
in Greece an old man mourn-
ing for the island he was born on, torn
between life and death,
his soul yearning for olives ripening in the sun,
where the wind on his neck is the breath
of a god. The world must be a temple.
Or a sacred theater,
a space dedicated to Dionysos,
sensual as the sea. Tell
the future his story, he implores you, what he's done
with his life. What loss
is. How the end when it comes is a silent disaster.

2.

Men drowning quietly out of sight,
wind blown, hawk's cry,
broken shells, a night
sleepers wake startled by the sight of a sky
white with gulls scattering before
the rising waves of a sea
that is breaking rocks into pebbles it discards on shore.

3.

Yes, words confuse things.
Nothing said is ever right. The keys
you hold in your hand no more
can open the locks that imprison
you. Sea gulls weakened
by wind, pelicans as storm-weary,
a wave-battered sailor.
Someone sings, a bell tolls.
How cruel laughter can be, mockery,
an ocean deriding you
where you stand on a boulder at land's end
studying an empty sky
like a child writing his name on a blank sheet of paper.

Tenebrae Factae ex Animo

1.

The shadows the moon casts through his window
on the ceiling. The silhouettes of trees
on a drawn shade in the morning, a row
of pine like a fence. In late spring, breezes

bringing maple seeds twirling, spinning,
flying into his room where they lie
on the floor, rug, his bedspread as if they're sleeping
with no earth to root in and so meant to die.

2.

He breaks his face in the lake with a stone.
The boy he watches stepping out of the surf
as if it were himself borne up, alone,
from the sea. The loamy smell of earth

on his body. What he's drawn to, lured
by. The dark he sees best in, unblinded
by light. The night inside him that assured
him he was right to hear what it said

about him. Friends forever, pledging
their lives together in a kind
of marriage, like lovers. The simple ring
it gave him to wear he didn't mind

was invisible. The sketch in charcoal.
he made of that boy and hid. The caves
by the lake he'd explore. The steep knoll
he'd tumble down till dizzy. What saves

a boy until he grows older is his fidelity
to the dark within him. What cannot lack
from his hiding inside it. Night's constancy.
The one lover he knows will always come back.

3.

Winter in the air, the ever-present thunder
of storm clouds, a chill bleak season,
fearful in a way, but wonder-
ful, too, defying sense, betraying reason,

the sun shining steadily on snow, burning
the earth to a cold, brittle brightness.
To have gained nothing, to know nothing
after so long a lifetime, to have to confess

to himself all he is becoming weary, tired of,
his heart chill as frost, as ice.
Solitude like December's, a northern love
like an Arctic darkness, the just price

he has paid, the debt he owes to night,
the gratitude to the one friend he has known
who has never left him. Tenebrous bright-
ness of a nocturnal heaven, stars bone-

white like snow, sky like the shadows
thrown by a man walking slowly across
a winter field at day's clos-
ing, at the world's darkening. The loss

of all sight save in the gloom of a black
night what is staring back at him, a dying
man who is leaving no trace, track,
or footprint behind him. No one, nothing

to be remembered by except for the shutters
he has demanded be closed, bookcases
emptied, drawers, closets, cabinets,
the unseen deeds, the unattended places.

4.

He is a tedious man, he knows, morosely afraid
of failing all feelings, of becom-
ing increasingly listless and staid,
coldly dispassionate, mutely numb.

Dread is like death inside him. No fear
ever leaves him. Nor does dark-
ness depart from him, though it is dear
as sleep. Shadows that left their mark

on him discolor, faint, disappear
so that all he is is what he is losing,
his mind in pursuit of a foolish dare:
that night might fall at more than fate's choosing.

5.
Oh, dark companion of his childhood,
he is saying goodbye to you as he fades
like evening, remembering how good,
how kind you were to him, the shades

drawn as he watches the moon shine
through, not its light that can matter
most but the specter you throw like a sign
on his bedroom ceiling. No dark could blur

your boyish face even as you must dance
above his dreaming, inviting him to join
you, swaying as curtains do, entranc-
ing him, inducing shivers in his loins

as he feels in his heart a burning, a longing
for night, for you, old stranger, a shadow
flickering like candlelight on the ceiling,
or, through a window, the moon's dimming glow.

What a Man Believes, So He Is

1.

Unrelenting, frigid, winter rain,
tempestuous winds for weeks
on end pounding on roofs, rattling windows.
A prolonged, storm-like pain,
its mute insistent shadows'
faces clearest where the cracked ceiling leaks.

2.

Pungent fragrances are scenting the air
with incense from a shrine to Buddha
his next door neighbors take care
of, honoring the gods. They've been reading the Gita,
would drift freely like a spirit floating over
the world, lie still as a rock under roiling water.

3.

At the beach, the salty air smells too near a kin
to the stink of a disemboweled crab
or discarded fish heads. Waves drench the skin
and fur of a half-flayed otter.
Hazardous riptides. Another drab
day, mountains, horizon a misty, faithless blur.

4.

To be baptized, cleansed by the sea again.
At the shoreline, to be freed of all fault,
purified by sun and ocean, wind and rain.
To delight in the clash of currents, thrill
to mutability, changeable skies. To exalt
in weather, the seasons as if joy is obedient to their will.

More than Watchmen for the Morning

1.

Low clouds like hills dawn has painted
yellow, rose, tawny orange, lavender.
The ocean sparkles like moonlit snow.
Crows peck at trash. Scavengers
search in bins for cans and bottles.
Night comes as promised, like waiting
all day for storms to begin. Wisps of fog
drift skyward like smoke from a fire.

2.

This is the year of the eighteen thousandth
sunrise since he departed from
his country to journey a continent
over mountains, past deserts, through cities
of men's discontent. He sits high above
the bay on Indian Rock, an exile
in an indigent place. Far below, at anchor,
cargo ships, small as decoys, wait to dock.

3.

Where is the dove that would fly him home?
Blond hair grown bald, nattering of old times,
he cups his hands, performs his morning
ablutions. A red dawn day. Leaves battering
windows in the breeze. Waves slapping
on cliffs. He recalls a lamb lost from its herd,
found dead, its skin flayed and stretched to dry
he saw while he changed a tire in Arizona.

4.

Night, then. The expected moment that comes
as a surprise, his bright eyes blackened
by solitude, dreaming of ancient byways,
of an island lying under a Mediterranean
sun. Ibiza. Mallorca. Or Rhodes. Patmos.
Hoping news might arrive millennia late.
Where the sea magnifies the sun without
any shadows and light seeps into caves and clings.

5.

Or to make a pilgrimage into sacred interiors.
To be stunned by mountain peaks, a cathedral
dome glowing from sunset's blessing,
not afraid though alone in Guanajuato,
far from his northern childhood home,
from its snow, ice, comforts, the peace
of ice on a lake, short days bracingly cold,
deep woods, birch forests keeping him warm.

6.

The stranger that is old age, its alien's
contorted, decrepit body, its broken promises.
He is a sailor abandoned by his ship
in enemy lands, onto a coast
where he is waiting for a boat he knows
won't show, for a sign he keeps anticipating
despite his knowing it will never arrive yet spies
at first light in white clouds that billow like unfurling sails.

A Priest, Unbeliever, on Easter

The moon's burnt orange, a harvest moon
in the middle of April. Tonight's the seder.
In four days, the crucifixion.
Rain and more rain. It is intemperate weather
for spring here. A cold
wind from a distant fog bank blows
toward shore. Our deaths are foretold
by time with a certainty, though no one knows
why. Moon, oh wettest moon,
oh Christ, why do you wait
so late to rise on this dark night? Soon
my fate will come when I'll be undone, the date
that obsesses me. I eat. I drink. My emptiness
is a meal like yours, Lord. Who took me as a lover love meant to possess.

An Oblation

A crisp chill wind. Dawn's light
this morning is so strong it stays
golden for hours as if it belonged
to the air, drenching it.
Flocks of gulls delighting in gliding,
celebrating day's
beginning, dipping, soaring,
circling back and forth,
then flying away,
carried by wind,
their feathers whether white
or dull brown
sun-lit to a jewel-like amber.
The headland
blazes with a pentecostal blessing,
a storm's long night
having cleansed the skies
while receding tides pounded the sand
so flat and slick it glares like burnished steel.
The sea is a lotus-
like lavender blue,
the waves' yellow-tinted fingers
its stamens on fire.
Ravens strut on driftwood black as priests.

Jesus of the dunes,
of burgeoning spring,
of early May,
when is it not good to honor your rites?
The sun, the honey-colored sun,
pours out its light
like wine for libation.
It is a dawn
whose radiance
I pray to stay drunk on.

A Renegade Priest to His Parishioners on Easter

He hangs on the cross still,
the wild, kind
man who cured the sick,
fed the hungry,
forgave sinners,
opened the eyes of the blind
of body or spirit.
All are one family,
he said. The ill.
Those in despair.
The dying. The dead. Mourn them we must, we
who were made from dust
for mercy's sake.
What prayer
should we say
to rectify
mistakes?
If it is our fear
of death
that makes the world holy,
then the world is holy.
The holiness that is you, my dear.
I'd enter the empty
tomb of your days
and cry to friends
waiting outside,
call to them,
"Come see,"
and leave them all stunned,
confused as Mary.

The Adoration of the Shepherds by the Le Nain Brothers

No stable, but a marble ruin more Greek
than Roman. Broken Doric columns,
ivy twined or dangling from them.
A donkey impassively waits behind

Joseph. Mary's adoring her baby, meek-
ly kneeling, her shawl a dark plum-
skin black. No sheep. One cow, nuzzling him,
the swaddled baby whose face looks resigned

to his fate. An old shepherd
leans on his staff. By his side,
a girl and a younger boy stand, probably his children,
their bodies partially hidden by their father's.

All are silent, worshipful in their way and so word-
less. Two angel children provide
a glimpse of heaven, the girl in pale pink, not vermillion
like Mary, the boy in drab green, his cloak's colors

the same as the shepherd boy's who wears a hat
like an upside down bowl. He could be the older brother
of the angel. Strangely, neither
attend to the infant, but are staring out of the frame.

What is so amazing, astonishing to them that
it distracts their gaze from Jesus? A light brighter
than incarnate god's? A far greater
miracle? A glorious something, whatever it might be, aflame

in the distance? No mat-
ter. It is an unseen splendor
their eyes direct the viewer
toward, a wonder they're still looking for.

IV

Maine

The island is a massive stark boulder,
a lavender cast to its snow cover,
sharp edges of jagged rock exposed
round a thin shoreline.
Flat white clouds gather
in a hazy sky, the water
a dark Prussian blue. Exposed
to sunlight, it glitters, shin-
ing with a satiny sheen. Black and spare,
two rowboats, their two men
working on nets, keenly aware
of how cold the water
is, how thin
the catch will likely
be since, despite the morning sun,
the sky
is darkening at the horizon,
threatening rain or sleet by noon.

2.

Woods in summer, thickly
canopied. Dense green moss
and weeds on unbroken ground.
The trees' and bushes' leaves weave together
in a seamless tapestry,
a burnished golden gloss,
gilt-brilliant, a flower-
y yellow shining like sun off water.
The forest's hush is the sound
of a world emptied of people. A break
in the foliage
opens to water more blue
than the sky, a hill
that gently dips to
a crystalline lake,
falls spill-
into it, and a boy and his toy boat waiting to make
their maiden voyage.

Woodlands, a True Story

Woodlands miles from home, backcountry,
a blue, shiny lake, a cabin abandoned
in the war
from which I still pilfer images
as if mine to keep. Photographs, calendars, muddy
shoes, yellowed letters, an earthenware
jar. It's in the flailing heat of summer's end
I hike through hickory,
oak, over grassy ridges
toward a clearing. Far off thunder, more than scary
to a kid. Damp humus.
Slippery red clay.
Thickets of vines to rip
past, brush to push
my way through, kudzu and honeysuckle.

That is how my life began, the first day
of it. Moccasins slithering
through water, skaters zigzagging,
gnats darting, rush-
ing aimlessly about as gusts grow fiercer,
birds circling
the lake while they struggle
to fly in strong winds, diving,
blessing the water as angels might do with a dip
of their wings, the sharp, peppery
odor of resinous pine.

All this, this world is little
more than air and dust now,
like the aftermath of a storm's big blow
that felled the oldest trees
by the edge of the meadow.

Yet in every sip
or breath I take it's in me,
the taste, the smell
of it, the rustle of leaves, the snap of twigs
as he steps toward the bank,
hunkers, drinks,
his uniform filthy,
rank,

his too long hair the color
of khaki, and limps off,
restored to the forest,
the wounded soldier
I've spied on, handsomely tall,
drinking while locust whirr
nearby, crickets chirp
beside him, birds swirling overhead
in a backcountry
a boy was too young, too small
to hike so deep into, yet stirred
into longing by
its trees, brush, high grass,
late August's darkly clouding, lovely sky.

And now I, still,
am bound to woodlands,
to its pine, oak, beech stands,
belonging to that place,
the groves, the hills,
the limestone caves I hid in,
each a part of me
as his memory
is for me as well a desire to see
on my body
his wounds, his face
as it was mirrored by the lake I stared into,
its calm untroubled water lit
afterward
by twilight
as evening winds made new waves
bending the reeds,
the weeds I stand in yet
since all I write, that's mine,
repeats no more than this: this glimpse
I had of him
on the first day of my life.

A Boy to the Old Man He's Been Changed Into

On the Jersey shore, no more than ten or so,
I'd wake earlier than anyone else and run
to the Atlantic's edge to catch the sunrise
and recklessly dive in, the surf enticingly wild.

Day's breaking was for me then, as you well know,
a kind of glory, a hope promised me by a sun
so bright it might have blinded me. But dawn never lies
to a boy, nor can sunlight deceive a child.

Water and sky and sun and the future. To whiff
the scent of seaweed on my body after swimming. Desire,
my flesh alive with it, surprising and new
like the surprises sand hid, the coins and toys I found.

Today, the sky and ocean are a smoky gray as if
somewhere far from here the earth is on fire.
Two black cargo ships slip silently through
high waves that batter their decks, both bound

for China. Abandon you? I do what I must do.
Stubborn, sad old man. Wave as I leave without you.

Nocturnal after Britten after Dowland

1.

On a starless night, slipping through
fog near the northwest horizon, a cargo
ship is so massive it might be a chunk
of the headlands that broke off or an ice
cap from the Arctic drifting in the Pacific.

While lying in bed, asleep, you are dreaming
of lives widely scattered by the sea.
You are a scavenger confused by what it has tossed
onto the beach, driftwood, bone shards,
sea-smoothed shells, sludge-blackened stones.

2.

Childhood sounds invade your rest,
locusts hissing, cicada crackling,
moths buzzing against screens,
the white noise of a radio at night
after the station has gone off the air.

Tonight, waves are breaking louder
than a crush of cars and trucks
rushing down the highway. Winds rattle doors
and window panes. This is what sleep
sustains. This disquiet. This restless music.

Franz Schubert, Vienna, November 18, 1828

1.

Curlews, choughs, swifts, blackbirds
alight like a single flock by tulips
near a rustic clock, its hands stilled
by the music of time. A scene without words
he is dreaming of. Off rooftops, rain drips
from a May storm. Dirt roads filled
with muddy pools. A papery white sky.
Birds resting on a garden's wet,
lushly green grass, its flowers
colorful, what little his eye
can see of them, petals claret,
burgundy red, butter yellow. Lures
for bees. Or tiny worms and mites
that gnaw and bite. All sing to him. Sing die.
Sing why he dreams of spring on this of all nights.

2.

He sits up in bed sweating in a poorly heated,
clammy room. Outside, breezes break
through the monotony of dying, sighing through a window
a friend opened when he had begged him to.
His sheets are sputum stained. Cheated
of life by an invisible worm for the sake
of a spasm. It is late in the evening.
Too many notes have gone missing
in each bar he has been composing, a lack
in his brain like the absence
of God. He is a ghost in sunlight, a shadow
in shade. If he could come back,
his soul re-inhabit a body, that miraculous feat,
he would be like his unfinished Lazarus: the silence
of scores he had had to leave, perfect and incomplete.

For Gerald Coble by the Battenkill

1.

Fragments of farms, their plots patches of crazy
quilt patterns and colors. A brushed passage like trees
defining a horizon, a swatch of greenery,
of bare branches stark as veins in leaves.
Or pyramids. Antique photos wrapped in string.
Collages. Gloves. Thorns. Thread spools. Primavera
in negative, its gods and their dancers juxtaposing
a red zipper strip, buttons bursting from the frame bolder than Flora.

2.

For decades, he's lived beside a river,
a wind and water world. Winter snow,
woods night deep. Landscape is a book
eyes write. The insights of place. What is there
to see, to be part of. A river's flow-
ing is as still as art is if you stop it to look.

3.

Drawings of a winter river and moon, a series
in two books. The right page: a lunar circle,
a rectangle the river runs through. Much
is left empty. The other: blank except the lower
far corner, a stamped imprint of two pods, peas
crisscrossed. A calligraphic brushwork, lyrical
as poems from the Tang dynasty. The deft touch
of ink on paper. Fluent moon and changing river.

4.

What is unseen are the trees on the other side
of its bank, a railroad track, more woods, a farm,
or a path leading down from the house to the water,
stones, sculptures, a barn. Just moon and river.
As if there is a light in the eye day has denied
that night knows. All things flow. Yes. And do no harm.

For Bill Miller (1921-1995)

You might have seen him. You might have passed by
him strolling down Fifth Avenue. Like others,
you might have crashed into a tree and not known why
or hit the stone wall along Central Park. As his lovers
would, they said, drunk on his looks. Or stood
beside him at the MET, staring at the same
Greek sculpture or black figure vase. You could
have sat near him at the Oak Room when he came
there to drink with George. More real than life, the past,
its archives of longing. Gaze at his photos. The most
beautiful man who has ever lived. Looks cannot last.
Everyone knows that. But desire is not so easily lost.
He walks close by you on Madison near Seventy First,
long dead, the hunger you need to have fed, the reason you thirst.

Forms of Worship

Even as my old parents grew frail, they would still walk
on a dirt trail that meandered beside a shallow brook
in woods near their home. They were quiet, did not talk
much as the old often don't. At path's end, an oak
tree waited, an ancient giant, in a grove made mostly
of maple and dogwood at the edge of a public park.
Once there, they would wait a moment, then, like a devotee
touching an icon, carefully place their palms on its bark.

Today, I saw two young women walking the median
by The Great Highway. At Lawton Street, they laid
their hands on a sign and turned back, a rite they began
long ago and each day observe for good luck, they said.

Lay hands on a tree. Touch a sign as if it were magical.
Keep liturgies of an ordinary need. Dare to be ceremonial.

Metaphysics

Coyotes nightly menace the western edge of the park.
The sea's beating against a new cement barrier.
A child was saved from the Pacific's icy water
late this afternoon. In the gathering dark,
raccoons squabble on a Chain of Lakes island.
Ravens squawk. Gulls cry. A wailing
drunk rails against God, tosses sand
in the air, accosts tourists at Judah
and La Playa while they are waiting
for the last N-train. A metaphysics
of mist. Street lamps glowing a silvery gray
that surpasses moonlight. A shopping cart unseen as it clicks
by on the sidewalk. A crow or someone who's hungry
invisibly scrounging through trash. Fog like rain in its clarity.

On a Beautiful July Day by China Beach

A young man has just jumped off the Golden Gate Bridge
from its eastern side. Tourists gape down at the water.
A red chopper, flying below it, hovers between
the pylons, searching for his body. An ambulance,
blocking lanes, waits, gurney out. Any high ledge
is a seductive spot. The problem is, isn't it?, the bother
suicide causes others. It is better done unseen.
Or a fall performed so artfully it looks like a loss of balance.
Fifty or more black-bellied plovers
gather on the beach, still as stones
for a moment or silhouettes in a play.
Suddenly, the flock flies off, as if travelers,
mere visitors here. Is this how the world atones
for pain? It's a lovely day to leave it. Why stay?

The First Day of The Outside Lands Concerts

The beach's cold and misty as a Maine
coast's winter. Dozens of geese and pelicans
stand on their shadows, the sand rain-
glazed at low tide. Nothing happens.

What are they waiting for the water
to do? Five young people rise out of dunes,
blankets draped like capes over
their shoulders, wrapped round them like cocoons.

The concerts begin tonight in the park.
They are bedraggled, hopeful, poor,
must crash through fences after dark
when the wind blows hard as off a moor,

ruffling the feathers on ravens' backs,
necks, revealing their scrawny bodies.
The kids pick up their paper sacks,
stretch their arms, wipe sleep from their eyes.

Loose sand blows off the shore and over
the highway, coating tongues, stinging
skin. They hesitate, frown as if fear-
ful they'll not be able to hear the singing,

the bands, the groups they have hitched so far
to follow. A blinding fog has fallen
on the Sunset. The N Judah streetcar,
clanging its bell, moves slowly, surely an omen.

Thousand thousands here for the superstars,
the gods of rock in the park. No surety
in this weather, though, like what gets said about wars.
No truth in the fog of it, only more folly.

A red-tailed hawk perches on a lampost,
head cocked to heed the right signs, eager for meat.
That is all they need to believe, or almost
all. Their ears must hear, their mouths must eat.

But what if these kids cannot get in, fail
to penetrate the gates? See no bands?
Shiver instead in their blankets in gale-
sharp winds, for warmth holding hands?

A wasted trip, the long journey lost?
Or would they huddle in the cleft of a dune
listening like children, star-crossed
children, to music as if it were being played on the moon

in the faraway park surrounded by chain-
link fences, kept out with no money
for tickets? Or through the mist, thick as rain,
would they hear a song in fog, in the cold of each day?

Suppose what is faint, vague, hazy is the only clarity.
What is dimly seen, not easily heard.
How I need to tell you what you mean to me.
How I long to name it and cannot find the word.

In the Last of the Thousand Lands

Haltingly, an old woman is walking
far from home. The road
is muddy in the early spring.
Husband, children are dead. The load
on her back is like a bag of sorrow.

Snow is slowly melting in a meadow.
Birds peck at seeds in a tree.
A farmer is plowing fresh land,
the just turned field rust-tawny
where sliced and sheared. A stand

of birches. Faint mist. Pale sky.
The pebbles and rocks by her path
glisten like mica. Such beauty
she sees, though mindful of death,
stones sparkling like stars. A crow

looks glad it is time for sow-
ing. Green sprigs are like dreaming,
like dawn ever-shining, limbs
stripped of ice, newly blooming,
the pungent woods, the hymns

finches are singing. The forest
is where she must wearily go
to reach oak, golden ash, the rest,
the sleep she is seeking, to know
what trees know, the roots below

her feet, the ground like a window
she spies through. To walk
through years frightened, then catch sight
of loveliness. She watches a hawk
fly like an arrow through white

clouds toward a garden of camellias,
dahlias, irises, roses—
like a lover's last flowers she's
been given as day fast closes
to evening's shade and shadow.

No more grief. Weeping. Sorrow.
It is the thousandth land
she has reached, journey's end.
"I'm tired," she says, and
waits for him, her dearest friend.

And he comes like solace to
an aged wanderer, to her,
Imagination, to who-
ever is a traveler,
who wishes life might bestow

on her today or tomorrow
before it is too soon over,
a vision of woods, plowed
fields, birds, clear water,
flowers, blue skies endowed

by grace of nature, by which
I mean by hope, dream,
desire, all the rich,
sweet mind conceives of that might seem
more real than dying if art could make it so.

V

The Twilight of His Early Years

Earth was paradise enough, a happiness present in everyday
pleasures. May elated him.   Why study? Its warmth'd melted
the ice and snow that late April had spared in its shadows.
Rogers Woods, Root Glen glowed from within, the way
forests will at dawn past a night's soft rain. His Vespa toot-tooted
down paths, through the college's trees, brookside willows,
sycamores, maples, oaks, and birches, with me riding behind
him, holding on tight round his waist since traces of winter's
dangers lingered in slick patches of cinders and mud.
Pastel green leaves, a trail of yellow dust like sand you find
on beaches, a blue sky whose clouds billowed with showers
to come, the linen-white lilac, dewy trillium, crocus in bud.
We lolled on the quads' rolled lawns, dozing, dreaming till
the sun boldly reddened, a twilight unending in that springtime still.

December, 1962

After Thanksgiving in '62 the trees, the streams,
fields, quads, hills, turned to white. In dreams,

we'd been made a promise that couldn't be kept: the snow
would melt early that year if, in the cemetery below

the chapel, the men, boys, a few women from the College,
slept undisturbed, no one joining them by the edge

of the campus. The roads ash-gray, covered with cinders,
the walk ways, coal black, it was the worst of winters,

the drifts piling head high as early as mid-December.
The crash happened before the break, Kit, Cam, Winger

(though Tom survived it), a pile-up in a blizzard
on the New York Thruway. A slash, a sudden fissure,

a rupture between worlds. The snow was rafter-high
around the Sig House after Kit's funeral. Irony,

our way of life, became useless. His mother, father
in the middle of a circle of his real and frat brothers,

their girls, all quiet. No one knew what to do or say.
Fresh snow shone like May into the room, the day

outside brilliant, icy white, a blue-cast
to it, a clear, close light like spring's. It didn't last.

The next night, a blast felled the tallest tree
in Root Glen. From a window in South Dorm, I could see

it fall. I watched how it died. The snow below it
exploded, then drifted back down. The big elm, split

apart by the wind's force, was buried under
a pall of white and disappeared. A trick of winter

is to make you feel safe inside, a fire
burning in the hearth in your room. Cam Myer,

Kit Miner, dead at twenty. The snow wouldn't quit
the night they were killed. The truck driver who hit

their car couldn't see it. It was invisible, like nothing,
a white out. Bright as sun on ice, his headlights, shining

on a snow pile, blinded him. Or blame absence,
winter's early dark, its cold, its silence.

Herkimer Dolomite

1.

Hunched, arthritic, his clothes reeking from
cigar smoke, an old man visits the Sig house
bearing tweeds, an itinerant tailor who sews
suits, jackets, slacks for young gentlemen,
his fabrics woven only from highland wool,
he says, their colors a subtle heather, thistle,
loch blue. No buyers. He shrugs. Times change.
He stacks his goods in the back of his coupe,
drives down College Hill Road, his cloth bolts
lined up like rolled up banners behind his seat.
Twilight late in January, the sky's bronze as if
rusted by age, a lustrous deep coppery brown,
like decaying leaves or the campus's gothic
buildings, their stones smoldering in near dark.

2.

Its deep pits are quarried out. What rock's left
to mine is ironless, won't rust, stays dull gray
through years of weathering, not worth cutting
into blocks to fix what's chipped or cracked
on the college's ancient edifices, stained by
two centuries of northern New York ice storms.
I first saw them in spring, boys playing lacrosse
in the quad by the chapel, the morning light
casting the dorms with a ruddy patina, sun
soaked, like the mid-May tan on the guys
pitching, catching the ball with their racquets.
Odd how vividly I recall them that one time,
three months before I enrolled, like a picture
revisited in a year book, as clear to me now

as October's glory days, the Mohawk Valley's
dense woods turning to bloody maroon,
scarlet, flare red, fiery gold, flickering
yellows like a shrine's votive candles, hearth
flames slowly dying to November embers,
ash pale or flake white. Winter began soon
as a day or two after each Thanksgiving,
a few trees left clinging to no more than
a swatch of leaves, losing them by the first
snow, the sky watery gray like smoke from
a dampened fire. In upstate, winters are hard,
long like those in Arctic zones. But the old
hewn blocks thrive in cold. Their colors
deepen, blushed by the rust burning in stone.

3.

Michelangelo carved to free bodies lost,
hidden, forgotten in marble. He knew
stone memories endure way past our own.
Too many to name them all, profs, friends,
but I'll risk a few: Crossett, Teddy, Lady
Ed, both Cams, Kit, and you I loved most,
though we seldom talked the days we could–
the boys, men dead as always before,
their spirits chill as College Hill winters.
No matter the season, the buildings glitter
like crystalline snow. But their sparkling façades
hide rock's deep veins. Say life also rusts
like iron to a color bronze as late Brahms.
A quarried music. Our mineral companion.

After Hearing News of the Deaths of More of My College Classmates

1.

The sea's in its summer season
here, thrumming, drumming its
rhythms on the shore.
A pelican, a raven,
a red-tailed hawk, just those three, no more,
sweep through the fog. A man sits
on a bench, trying to sleep,
his clothes filthy and torn.
He reeks of pot and alcohol.
Mist is seeping deep
into a silent city. A fog horn
mourns through the Golden Gate. If only all
men and women
might lie in their beds at rest
free from grieving while each dreams
of tomorrow. On the beach, a dozen
snowy plovers, skittering on the sand, are blest
with plentiful worms from retreating tidal streams.

2.

Woods' half-light,
humus, decay
underfoot, the worn, leathery smell
of damp bark, the height
of the tallest trees
frightening when day
grows almost dark as night,
ivy thickets, the swell
of creeks in spring, wild
flowers blossoming, a breeze
shaking leaves, nuts that fell
with a cracking sound on the forest floor,
a child
long ago lost in the depths of it,
deliberately gone missing, sore
from hiking so far in, sit-
ting on a boulder, alone,
pondering fragments of a lichen-bearing bone.

3.

Winter on College Hill,
the steep climb back up
from the Tavern, the Inn,
the flakes you'd cup
in your gloves, the thrill
of real cold, the thin
light of the chapel
through the flurries,
its bell intoning each quarter hour,
classes, studies
the next day, an icy shower
waiting before bed while far away,
near the woods, Colin Miller's son's play-
ing his bagpipes, its plaintive music
strange on such a crisp night, like mourning
too soon, like a trick
of time, you think, reaching
your frat house, the guys inside still busy partying.

La rêve de l'aurore du petit Pierre

1.
Argenteuil, its bridge over the Seine, pink-gray clouds hastening through the heavens, racing their own fleeting shadows darkening glen, meadows, dimming poppies' scarlet blossoms, lupine, lilies, white and yellow daisies. Migrating swifts flying from trees, gliding, circling above their leaves. Salmon splashing upstream, silvery minnows flashing through reeds. A barge towing two skiffs. The silvery sound of breezes at dawn rustling through tall weeds.

2.
The lawn's newly shorn grass is tickling his back as the little boy stares at the last of the morning's rack of clouds, vast as blimps, passing over France. Spring winds are blowing them toward the far Pyrenees, the water below his feet flowing, dancing spritely, glistening from a re-born sun. All he sees is drifting, ever-changing, shifting speeds, fast, slow, fast.

3.
It is a bewitching dawn, an enticing start to his day as the last stars fade. The earth, the sky, the light, the air, the unbearable reality of everything he sees making him close his eyes. To fantasize. To recall the sweetness of the time that arrives just before waking.

4.
The paper boat he made and played with yesterday is floating away, drifting out of sight. It pleases him to watch it go. What matter if he already knows that no one, nothing stays here forever. It pleases him to see it vanish.

5.
Like fabled Ys into Bretagne's sea, his life will sink and drown beneath its waves, waiting there to be resurrected, like a city restored, perfected by water's promise, by streams and rivers, by what the Seine pours into the sea to rise out of history's flood, its vast tides. So too he, petit Pierre. And his family. And all that abides in the air after showers.

6.
He wakes in his apartment in Paris from a dream of morning when he was a boy in Argenteuil. The light through the window refracted by an empty glass he had set on the sill late last night colors his sheets. His lover lying beside him strokes his forearm, kisses his cheek. Oh, sunlight breaking through mist painting the sky with its famous arc. The thrill a child feels from any kept vow, to be able to say like the dawn to tomorrow, "Again, my dearest, again."

Two Boys in Room 107 in The Longleaf Pines Motel off Route 421

1.

Everything is strange, what is happening between them, new, scary, the sleazy, cheap motel room they have booked where no one asks questions that smells of shower stall mildew, or, worse, a fetid bog, an algae-covered frog pond, the stink when it hits their noses sickeningly pungent yet which as best they can they ignore, left unlooked into, unexplored, swear is unimportant as boys used to such things might have sworn.

2.

This moment, this meeting, is urgent for them both, like telling the truth for once, despite the fact the room is a shambles, window shades frayed, glasses left shattered against a wall, ashtrays scattered on the floor, a ripped and yellowed sheet strewn in pieces on a torn rug, the one table lamp, when lit, no brighter than a candle. Headlights from the highway sneak in like eyes peeking through the shutters' slats.

3.

On the double bed's unmade mattress, sweaty, not yet completely naked, his shirt unbuttoned, his exposed chest boyishly hairless, older, seventeen, he is waiting for his first kiss on his lips, wary, uncertain perhaps because it is the first time for both of them to make love like this, in a bed, in a darkened room as if nothing but it were real.

4.

His friend is moving slowly, carefully closer over the sheets, his eyes focused solely on him as the room grows dimmer when he clicks off the lamp with the party hat shade on it. The younger boy almost cries he is so happy, the bed a little damp, already wet in spots from their bodies' heat after his friend has tugged off his boxer shorts, he his briefs, a delirium of sorts mounting between them, passionately embracing until the boy, smiling, awkwardly puts his hand on him where no one has touched him before, the deep, certain pleasure of it, his mind racing wild, thoughts drifting off, the sweetness of it, maybe unrepeat-able, never to be known again.

5.

The tenderness afterwards, both lazily lying wrapped in one sheet in a room desperation or history has led them to. Lights still off, the stain of their love-making seeps into the bed, completing their joy, the sign of it, the left-behind trace of a bliss as mysterious as grace is, as happiness is, a blessing one soon learns one should not try to explain, what lasts past darkness enduring in wonder.

6.
And you, in London, writing me all these years later, no other words from you ever before, asking if I still remember.

The Colonels Greece

1.

The cloudy sky is a faded linen gray. The sea is rippled like slabs of marble or, by the cliffs, is a green shiny as olive leaves. Waves break and tumble in, wind tossed on a fitful day. Graffiti has been whitewashed on boulders, protests scrawled on posts attacking the fascists in Athens. Tragedies are common, if tragedy is murdered sons, imprisoned fathers, cruel decrees, mothers' cries, raped daughters.

2.

His hair knotted and white, a ragged man hunts the beach for treasure, maybe a drachma, a fragment of a bronze statue, a bit off a chipped carved stone, or an ancient coin water has spared and spent on sand. What pleasure he seems to take in his pursuit must be real, like an explorer seeking a city lost to jungle or a diver a wrecked ship loaded with gold artifacts and bullion or remnants of a pirate hoard a storm took down.

3.

A gull on a cliff regards the old Greek warily. He knows no despair, this man I watch, discovering nothing, uncovering only tourists' trash, daring, free, talking to himself like some ancient in his olive grove, muttering about traitors perhaps or some love long denied him, no less fierce, no less rash than when young, alone with his incessant failure, digging with stick and thick, gnarled hands beneath the sand's fool's gold glitter as if it were something deep within earth he is hoping to find, a fragment more darkly true, however ruined, than his nation's raging dawn sun with its fiery tyrant's eye burning through weak clouds like paper.

4.

"Why wander the beach a few more summers with my stick and dimming sight? Why wither like a vine on a stake? I have gone to meet my friend Cleisthenes and his two young sons in that land below which knows no betrayal but the only one none can resist."

Key West

1.

The hotel is abandoned, shut down. He locks the door to the lounge. Listening to storm reports, he washes cocktail glasses behind the bar. Each one he has dried, he places on a plastic shelf that runs across a mirror he refuses to look in, frightened by whom he might see at fifty-three, afraid to count the days until, one by one, they are all gone. Restless, he is waiting for a call but won't pick up the phone, numbering each time it rings as just one more he has to hear before it is really over between him and his wary boyfriend, his heart unable to bear another in an unending list of losses.

2.

The brutal winds shake the building, bouncing the bar's tables and chairs around as if an earthquake, not a hurricane were breaking the island apart. He tastes ash on his tongue and swills some Cuban rum he keeps stashed beneath the cash register. A hundred burning huts make their own storm he had learned as his best friend ran amuck after their platoon had lit them all, screaming he deserved a god damn medal some lieutenant had deprived him of, then shooting chickens, pigs, gooks before he blasted his head off his neck with a grenade that killed him and all the villagers that were still alive. Dennis survived, brought back from the dead in a field hospital while gripping his best friend's dog tags.

3.

He wears them around his neck like an amulet. After he has rinsed another glass in the soapless water, he wipes it with a fresh towel and inspects it for spots by the absinthe green light that fills the room as the winds increasingly seem to throb like a drum while burning the air inside him. The chain round his neck feels tighter than it has ever felt before, the tags weighing on his chest heavy as a shield. As he falls, he cannot pull them off quick enough. Is his zippo out of fluid? A bar mate hands him his own. For once, a hut burns fast as the enemy flees from the flames in his brain while their animals bellow and squawk.

4.

History is porous, like Florida soil. I watch the news, see the images of the Keys' near destruction in places, imagining him during the storm he did not survive decades before. How the heart attack that killed him in the midst of it was the outbreak of another war Dennis had never wanted to fight.

Queer Childhood

1.
Born in a forest, he is a boy raised
apart, a mute child
who would feed where sheep grazed,
whom a she-wolf, they say, turned wild,
who grows
more brute-like each day but can't disappear,
not a doe's
fawn but a wolf's cub who fears what wolves fear.

2.
Grandparents, parents, sisters, brothers—
all his family dead to him before he's nine,
buried in the cemetery
of his soul's silence, his dispossession sign
there are no others
like him among the children playing as snow falls on their city.

"We Love Life and Therefore Fear Death"

1.

Mike is standing by a cactus grove in Joshua Tree.
The sun in its generosity is burning
the wide world white. The sky is cloudless. To see
him is impossible in such ferocious glare. Like nothing.
Or the earth's disappearing at the end of days.
We have already said our goodbyes. He stares at me
and smiles, like an afterimage, an illusion that stays,
a lover lingering outside time, faithful to his beauty.

2.

Clouds shroud the headlands today. There is an art
to its clarity like Agnes Martin's, the way the hills yield
like paint to abundant light, to a luminosity that is part-
ly darkness, like the sun unveiling mist from an open field.

3.

One last, uncertain glimpse of earth is all I ask from dying:
to leave the life I love, forgiven and forgiving.

Equinox

Half light, half dark, dawn is hesitant.
Three surfers carrying their boards skip
on the beach toward the water.
A young man throws driftwood sticks
for his dog to retrieve. A boat with a searchlight
scans the waves, through the night persistent
in finding whatever it is looking for. Rip-
tide warnings are posted, the sea more danger-
ous when it is dark. The dog licks
his friend's face. A boy jogs out of sight
into dense fog at a bend in the coastline
where cliffs jut into the ocean at the end of the continent.
This must be what Catullus meant.
Run. Run
after him. Every day now there will be less sun.

To a Friend Who a Fundamentalist Christian Friend Said Was Doomed

A plank walkway leads to the estuary
where an incoming tide rustles reeds
and cattails growing out of a bog.
There is no moon. The sky is cloudy.
Early morning breezes blow through trees.
Thick weeds crackle like a fire as they shake.
It is a monkish solitude here where Douglas fir,
redwoods, ever-flowing tidal waters
are disturbed only by the rare rumbling
of semis traveling on Sir Francis Drake
carrying full milk cans and crates,
braking at the curve by an isolated shack.
At dawn, sunrise burns the hills,
scrub trees, and summer dry grasses
while to the south a billowing fog spills
over them like a tide refilling the sea.
More than a century ago, a vast crack,
plates clashing, forced this lay of earth
northward like an island broken off
from the mainland. It was violence
that made this good place. Neither birth
nor death: to know nothing, to understand
nothing but what is heard in its silence.
A heron is fishing in shadows of the vanishing dark,
a stick figure in silhouette, tall, stark,
quietly stalking its prey. It moves
so slowly it seems without motion.
Birdsongs, a waylaid long billed curlew's,
a sparrow's warbling, a junco's trilling.
Breaking day is awakening those still dreaming.
The tide is retreating to the Pacific ocean.
And the white heron, with a fish in its beak,
flies over reeds to a sand spit near where
the bay ends by Route One to disappear
from my spying eyes. What does it mean
to revere a bird? Dead fish, fed heron?
Or a slight, solitary, camouflaged snake, green
as the grass through which it slithers
toward shade away from day's dangers,
sparkling, dear God, like a diamond necklace
from the sunlight shining off its dew-slick scales?

Gilgamesh

1.

The surfers in their wet suits are puppets
in a shadow play. The sky is a gray
ceramic plate. The tumbling Pacific
is a Hokusai print, the beach a sandy
patch in a Diebenkorn Ocean Park.
The world looks flat as that, though it's
constantly changing. I heard a monk say
the world is the surface of a pool. What is thick
lies deep within it. Life floats on the stream of be-
ing. Sunlight glitters off what is dark.
I managed once in the Neuse's roiling
waters to touch bottom. To uproot a reed
to prove I had done it. But it was nothing.
Just mud. Silt. A river's slimy, rotting weed.

2.

Remember the chilly night that I watched you
standing immobile on a treeless hill
in west Marin, staring toward an invisible
ocean? The moon had set, the stars
were dim, and the sky, like your back,
black as the unseen sea or the bleak view
one gets of the universe, emptily still,
between galaxies. You looked like a marble
statue or a tall runic stone. What was ours
in such darkness? In the silhouette of your back
turned toward me as if you'd been cut
from the sky like a swatch of cloth? I wanted
to join you, knowing you were fading out
of sight into night that night we parted.

Goodbye

Maybe these woods. At least there are enough trees to declare
where the clearing starts, a brook snaking
through oak and maple groves to a lake. A meadow's
a childhood place, like a child's dreams
that, if you say so, dare
to come true, the future free for the taking.
The crosstown bus I'm riding goes
too fast. Suddenly, it's my stop. The driver beams
at me as I step off and wave goodbye. Poetry's
like that, a man who has pursued a city's
streets to freedom returning to a forest that sees
him approaching from far away. To memory's
streams fated to flow seaward. To the earth he couldn't know
how much he'd love when a boy played in a meadow, so briefly long ago.

Epilogue: To a Favorite Poet

Snow is what his poems mean, the surprising kind
coming in early spring gentler than winter's,
the earth still warm from yesterday's sun,
thawing so fast no harm is done to flowers.
Behind his house, high over a spruce forest
rises a craggy ice-capped mountain peak
the sun ignites each dawn like a match, struck
on rock, that the wind blows quickly out.
Such cold is what his poetry wants to say,
the strange chill of age from the day he was born,
the nip of fall in all he has loved, the words
of his work as if chiseled from ice. That crystalline.
That light, impossible to touch or hold, like sleet
to a boy's delight, melting in his hands.

CPSIA information can be obtained
at www.ICGtesting.com
Printed in the USA
BVOW03s1803241117
501179BV00005B/750/P